Life Changing Classics, Vol. XXXII

# The Seven Leadership Virtues of Joan of Arc

*Peter Darcy*

TREMENDOUS LEADERSHIP
Leadership with a kick!

Life-Changing Classics, Volume XXXII

# THE 7 LEADERSHIP VIRTUES OF JOAN OF ARC

Published by
Tremendous Leadership
PO Box 267
Boiling Springs, PA 17007
717-701-8159 800-233-2665
www.TremendousLeadership.com



Print ISBN: 978-1-949033-32-8
Ebook ISBN: 978-1-949033-33-5

# TABLE OF CONTENTS

# SYNOPSIS

Among history's leaders, Joan of Arc stands out as one of the pre-eminent figures. This small book tells the tale of her leadership virtues as a mystic and a warrior who obeyed the command of God to perform extraordinary deeds. Because of her virtue, she had a profound effect on both the earthly and heavenly kingdoms.

Among all the excellent qualities Joan of Arc exhibited in her short life, this book focuses on these seven: **spirit** (her spiritual formation and personal zeal); **identity** (her strong sense of self and personal calling); **power** (her excellent judgment in using coercive power to save her country); **mobility** (her purposeful action in executing her mission); **realism** (her ability to judge correctly what to do in complex situations); **attraction** (her immense powers of persuasion); and **inspiration** (the way in which she called the men and women of her day to heroism).

Although Joan of Arc lived six hundred years ago, she is a leader we should still learn from today.

# INTRODUCTION

The Bibliotheque Nationale in Paris contains numerous artifacts reflecting how the 15th century maiden named Joan of Arc captured the imagination of the world. According to one biographer, Mary Gordon, there are more than 20,000 books about Joan of Arc in that library alone. The sheer number of works about a medieval teenager defies imagination but speaks *volumes* about her singular contribution to human history.

The curmudgeonly Mark Twain was enamored of Joan. So great was his esteem for her life and accomplishments that he once said that it took six thousand years to produce a Joan of Arc, and the world would need another fifty thousand years before anyone of her stature would ever appear again. High praise from a man who did not dole out compliments lightly.

The scope of this endeavor will narrowly focus on one dimension of her life and character that had the greatest impact on the world: her leadership skills. Joan was not a politician, although she worked with many of the key political figures of her day. She made no direct contributions to culture, although European culture was tremendously enriched by her exploits. Joan of Arc was unabashedly a military leader of the French people as they took back their country from an invading army. She claimed no title except that of *Maid.*

Fine leadership skills are a rare trait, and it is unlikely that anyone is truly *born* a leader. Many people become good leaders through training but others, like Joan of Arc, have a certain God-given *charism* of leadership that enhances their natural skills for leading men and nations. In these rare instances, the individual's human formation, character, and circumstances add the rest. History has seen its share of great leaders and Joan of Arc, who did extraordinary things in such a short period of time, takes her place among them in one of history's fullest expressions of leadership.

Most shocking is that this world class leader had not yet reached the age of twenty when her leadership gifts were poured out as an offering for her fellow countrymen. The entirety of her "career" lasted less than a single calendar year.

By depicting in a few words and images the astonishing leadership virtues of Joan of Arc, we can only present seven inadequate snapshots of a life fully lived. We cannot go into much detail about her personal or family history, her extraordinary spiritual gifts, or even the shocking way in which her life was cut short by the traitorous leaders of her day. You will find a short list of superb resources for further reading at the back of this book and, of course, there are at least 20,000 other titles for your edification.

As a preliminary to this book's core essentials, it is well to present Joan of Arc's life at a glance through a brief factual summary of important historical details, names, and terms. This overview, though simplified, gives us a foundation for viewing the vast and beautiful panorama of one of the greatest lives ever lived.

My prayer is that you may be encouraged by these seven cameos of Joan of Arc and fortified by the example of her virtues in whatever capacity you are called to exercise leadership in our modern world.

# THE LIFE OF JOAN OF ARC

In 1412, a few decades after the Black Plague wiped out half the population of France, Joan of Arc was born in the northeastern corner of her homeland (the province of Lorraine), just east of where they produce Champagne today. Hers was a pious Catholic farming family and she was the fourth of five children, having three brothers and one sister.

Joan came into the world during an era of great social and political upheaval. England and France were three quarters of the way through the longest war in history, known as the Hundred Years' War. An uneducated young woman from a rural area of France was chosen by God to end it.

She accomplished this purpose by convincing the crown prince of France (called the *dauphin*), Charles VII, to appoint her as leader of France's military forces so that she could lift the siege of the city of Orléans and begin the liberation of her country from English domination. The French broke the back of the English siege on May 8$^{th}$, 1429, an event that is celebrated in the city of Orléans to this day. Joan was 18 years old when she did this, a deed for which she is known to history as "The Maid of Orléans".

Following the battle to save Orléans, Joan led the French army through 165 miles of English-held territory (all of Northern France) and liberated city after city in order to reach the city of Reims where Charles was crowned as King of France in the face of conflicting English claims to the throne.

After this culminating victory of her short career, the politicians of France and England engaged in a long, wasteful series of negotiations which sidelined Joan of Arc's immense leadership talents. The failure of these diplomatic efforts led to Joan's only military losses and her eventual capture at the gates of the city of Compiegne on May 23rd, 1430.

Joan of Arc was held captive for the next year and was eventually imprisoned in the medieval castle in Rouen, France (in Normandy), where she was subjected to a three-month trial by church authorities for witchcraft and heresy. In that era, church and state were not separate as they came to be in later centuries.

The English and their French partisans (the Burgundians) sought to use this trial to discredit her victories and thus also undermine the legitimacy of the French king. The trial remains one of the greatest acts of injustice ever recorded. Virtually every word of it was set down on paper, making Joan of Arc perhaps the most documented public figure in history prior to the modern era.

Joan of Arc was convicted of heresy and burned at the stake in the city square of Rouen on May 31st, 1431, at the tender age of nineteen.

The Hundred Years' War ended in 1453 with a victorious France completely free of English control. Soon after that (1456), the Catholic Church conducted an official review of the trial that condemned Joan of Arc twenty-five years earlier. The process, known as the Rehabilitation, completely nullified the original verdict of her condemnation. Joan of Arc's mother, Isabelle, formally petitioned the Rehabilitation at a ceremony in the Cathedral of Notre Dame in Paris and was still alive to witness its outcome.

The Catholic Church canonized Joan of Arc as a saint and a martyr in the year 1920, nearly five hundred years after Joan's life and deeds graced the earth.

# 1

## THE ANGEL

**Virtue: Spirit**

An angel is a purely spiritual being. There is nothing of flesh or matter in him. He does not live in the world but visits to communicate the divine will in special ways to God's servants. Every biblical account of an angel depicts a being who adopted human form for a specific mission but who does not live in time and space naturally as human beings do. The archangel Raphael made this theological point clear to Tobias when he explained that it only *looked like* he was eating human food (Tobit 12:19).

An angel was sent by God to Joan of Arc when she was about thirteen years old, and that encounter branded her with the seal of a spiritual mission. According to Joan's own account, Michael the archangel himself came to her when she was at prayer in the front garden of her family home. He was accompanied by a host of heavenly companions, and they were bathed in spiritual light. Archangel Michael didn't even take on human form for this encounter but appeared directly to her soul and senses in a vision.

Joan was unable to explain more than a few words about the encounter, as is common for people who claim to have seen heavenly beings. As a *mystical* experience, such encounters often escape description in words. However, when she was asked by one of her inquisitors if the glorious archangel had *hair and clothes* Joan burst into a fury. Her response to the rather silly question (from a cleric who should have known better) was the exasperation of a saint: "Do you think that God cannot clothe His own angels?!" That answer discouraged any further questioning about Joan's encounter with angels.

But the angel came with a purpose, and that was something Joan could explain to her questioners. In fact, she was very open about explaining the mission she was given by the archangel. It was this: *she was chosen to drive the English out of France and crown the king.*

## Spiritual Formation

Joan's encounter with an angel brings us to the question of the spiritual formation of a leader. It is an essential dimension of Christian leadership, which is why it appears first on the list of virtues enumerated in this book. There are three notable characteristics of Joan's spiritual formation by the angel; her spiritual foundation, spiritual willingness, and spiritual strength.

⚜ Foundation:

Joan of Arc was already a fervent believer in Christ and the mission of His Church by the time she met the angel. The archangel Michael didn't need to give her a course in remedial Christianity for her mission. There are those who are instructed and guided by angels (Abraham, Genesis 18); others who are prevented from doing evil by an angel (Balaam, Numbers 22); still others whose lives are dramatically transformed by angels (Hagar, Genesis 21; Tobias and Sarah, Book of Tobit).

When God sends an angel to enlist a soul for a particular mission, it is essential for the person to have a foundation of faith (like Joshua, Gideon, the Virgin Mary, John of Revelation) upon which to build the understandings and capacities needed for the mission.

Such was the foundation in young Joan of Arc whose parents were deeply pious believers and whose entire milieu was that of a profoundly religious culture. It is not surprising that the Arc family home stood only twenty-five or thirty feet from their parish church. Joan grew up in the shadow of the Church. She learned her catechism and embraced the moral and spiritual values that accompanied a faith-imbued society. On top of that, it was acknowledged by her own villagers that, even before she received her calling, Joan had a special attraction to prayer and things of the spirit.

⚜ Willingness:

Upon this strong personal spiritual foundation an angel was able to build a mission with a distinct clarity of purpose. The angel told Joan that she was the one whom God had chosen to do battle with the English. This was not as shocking a revelation to her as we might imagine. Her parents and her own French-partisan villagers were adamant that *someone* needed to drive those blasphemers out of holy France! (The French nickname for their enemy was *godon*, a mispronunciation of the term the English used when taking God's name in vain.)

Likewise, the need to crown the Catholic king of France in the ancient venue of kingly consecrations – Reims Cathedral – eventually became a personal *imperative* for the young faithful woman. This divine coronation mission that was later greeted by the intellectuals of the day with scoffing and derision was welcomed with a perfectly open heart by a faithful young woman, even if she had no idea how to implement the plans. That too would be directed by the angel in time.

⚜ Strength:

For nearly three years the archangel Michael appeared to Joan (together with two female saints,

St. Margaret and St. Catherine of Alexandria) to communicate to her the spiritual strength needed for the mission. We don't know Michael's methods, but his continuous driving home of the basic outlines of what needed to be done must have acted like an engraving tool etching in her soul a line of firm purpose that would never be undone by the pragmatic logic of prideful, worldly men.

We may also surmise that it was the mystical visions themselves that filled Joan with the strength needed for the battles ahead. For those of us who have never been gifted with spiritual experiences of the sort, this dynamic might be difficult to comprehend. Nonetheless, we have seen these mystical effects in other people who met angels: Abraham bowed down to the angels he met; Joshua took off his shoes on the holy ground consecrated by the angel; Daniel fell on his face and his companions fled in terror; John of Revelation actually wanted to worship his angelic messenger; the guards at the tomb of the Resurrected Christ *fainted*!

Like a trusted spiritual mentor, but vastly more so, the archangel Michael molded Joan's young soul with spiritual values to give her strength for her mission: divine enlightenment, robustness of soul, virtue, a clear perception of God's will, and all the gifts and fruits of the Holy Spirit that, by their very nature, angels share in a superabundant way. All of those graces flowed into the soul of an extraordinary young woman who sat at the feet of an angel for three years.

### Our Spiritual Foundation as Leaders

Few of us will ever meet an angel face to face, and if so, we are unlikely to be sent to save a whole country! In the same respect, the basic contours of Joan of Arc's encounter with the angel apply to us for our respective missions as leaders.

First, while God assists everyone on the road to heaven, His chosen ones usually have a strong spiritual foundation upon which to build a mission. If we have not been given good faith formation by our parents, family of origin, or culture, we can make up for the deficit by becoming fervent believers and members of faith communities that strengthen our faith. This is the function of the Church: to communicate the saving message of Christ to others and to form our souls in the Way, the Truth, and the Life of Christ (John 14:6).

Second, God's missions are only for the willing, and they are always the fruit of prayer. The Kingdom of God is vast and wide and always has a great need of workers for the vineyard (Matthew 9:39). Whatever the call to leadership entails or directs, our willing hearts allow God to work through us.

Likewise, clarity about God's will is the fruit of prayer. Yes, we should consult trusted counselors for discerning His will, but above all we must "beg the Lord of the harvest" to show us what He wants of us. In the Middle Ages people matured and entered into their vocations more quickly than today, so it is entirely believable that a young woman of thirteen or fourteen would already be seeking to know her path in life. This is why the archangel Michael appeared to her *in prayer*.

Finally, the many "angels" (role models) in our lives give us virtues and strength for our mission. What soul has not been inspired to greater faith by a truly holy person or some virtuous intervention of a righteous individual? Who has not been inflamed with love and hope by a fervent sermon or the witness of someone who has given his or her life to God's service?

Above all, we should pay close attention to the examples of leaders who are living the mission we wish to embrace. They or their personal stories have much to teach us even if they are not mentors in a direct sense. They are angels to us in a metaphorical sense, forming our souls, influencing our intellects, and inflaming our desire for righteousness. God uses the wealth of His spiritual and human faith communities to give us vigor for the mission.

Joan shows us that many types of "angels" are necessary for the spiritual foundation of a leader. Follow *your* spiritual mentors into your holy mission.

# 2

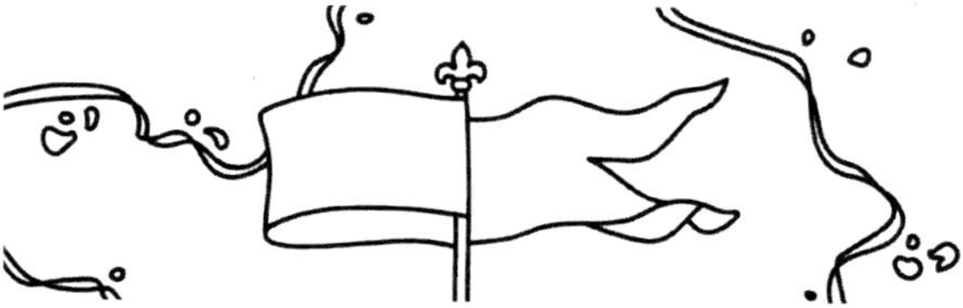

## THE BANNER

**Virtue: Identity**

It was twelve feet long, silky white, and emblazoned with the names of Jesus and Mary – a warrior's banner. It was mounted on a tall pole for all to see, the resolute declaration of a conquering hero like David of old: "You come against me with sword and spear and scimitar, but I come against you in the name of the Lord of hosts" (1 Samuel 17:45).

Thus did Joan of Arc ride into battle – holding high the banner, declaring her identity as a Christian soldier. Joan knew who she was and announced it to her friends and enemies alike. Such a bold, bright, obstinate declaration of a warrior's character must have struck mortal fear into the hearts of every foe, as the maiden clad in armor and fire rode onto the battlefield bringing war to their strongholds.

The English occupiers of France were so terrified by this banner, and the maiden carrying it, that they convinced themselves she had to be a witch. No woman had such power and authority on her own.

In that insight *alone* were they correct. Her authority was not her own but came from her identity infused by her God: certainly no witch ever identified herself with the holy names of Jesus and Mary.

### Joan's Core Identity

After her spiritual formation by the archangel Michael, Joan had no doubts about her core identity. She was the one called by God to drive out the English and to assure that her king was crowned at Reims Cathedral. Her angelic experiences left no doubt about what she had to do. She and the mission were one, and her banner acted as a sort of seal of confidence in the accomplishment of her mission.

Joan's identity was not only spiritual but had a cultural precedent, as all identities do. Everyone receives their human formation through communities that leave an imprint on their souls and characters for good or ill. In Joan's case there was a marvelous and mysterious medieval legend passed down by French society for centuries that played a powerful role in her self-understanding.

This pious legend, it is believed, had its roots in King Arthur's court many centuries earlier and made its way to France for reasons that will be obvious from its contents. The legend spoke of a maiden who would arise from a region in the eastern part of France (Joan was from the eastern province of

Lorraine) and would singlehandedly "fall on the backs of the archers" and vanquish them. These, at least, are the bare bones of the prophecy.

It is not hard to see how this legend came to be applied to Joan of Arc once she started making noises about driving the English out of France. The "archers" were the English longbowmen, the victory predicted was the eventual expulsion of the English usurpers from French soil, and Joan was the Maid from the east.

During her short career in the public eye, Joan referred to herself exclusively as "the Maid" (in French *La Pucelle*). Virtually everyone else at the time used that title for her as well. Few called her by her given name, Jehanne, and no one in her day ever used her last name, Arc, which was the surname of her father. She was *the Maid*, the one called by God (spiritual identity) and predicted by history (prophetic/cultural identity) to carry out the mission she had been given.

Let us acknowledge three notable characteristics of Joan's identity: symbolism, personal character, and ownership.

⚜ Symbolism:

Joan had an intuitive grasp of the value of symbolism in leadership. Symbols speak loudly about personal (and corporate) identity and endow what they symbolize with deep meaning. Joan cut her hair to symbolize the female warrior in the company of men. She wore armor to symbolize her oneness with her soldiers. She had priests lead the troops in processions before battles to symbolize the holiness of their mission. She dictated aggressive letters to demand the surrender of her enemies as well as pleading letters to her countrymen exhorting them to join the cause more fervently. What is a letter if not a symbol of a soul's thoughts and aspirations put down to paper?

Joan was masterful at communicating through symbols because she knew that human beings understand spiritual realities through symbols. Oftentimes the world of spirit has no other way to be understood. France, the land of soaring Gothic cathedrals and brilliant stained glass windows, taught its most celebrated daughter well.

⚜ Personal:

The Jesus/Mary banner was Joan's flag. Joan described its design to an artisan while at court waiting to begin her campaign for Orléans, and she even got the dauphin to pay for it! She also had a pennant and a guidon (flag to rally soldiers) made to assist the troops in times of war, but the white banner was hers, and it was very personal. Joan later testified that Michael the archangel gave her the specific design. Nonetheless, the historical record tells us that she carried it into every battle she fought. She also stood next to the king with it when he was finally crowned in the Cathedral of Reims.

The proliferation of logos, insignia, and paraphernalia for sports teams, celebrities, and businesses today may provide some insight into the very human need to declare our loyalties and identify ourselves with people and movements we greatly admire. Why should a medieval maiden have been any different?

⚜ Ownership:

Leaders are public figures whose lives and actions are under near-constant examination. Some measure of scrutiny comes with the very nature of public service or business. Consequently, leaders are often criticized, challenged, and even defamed for their actions and positions, and Joan knew every bit of that. She had her share of adulation as a conquering hero, of course – which poses its own dangers – but she knew disparagement up close and personal. The record states that the terrible epithets of the English (who called her a witch and a prostitute) were exceedingly hurtful. Her enemies eventually put her to death claiming, falsely, that she was a heretic.

Nonetheless, Joan owned her identity. No level of slander or praise could shake Joan's understanding of her divine calling or her fulfillment of the ancient prophecy. She was the Maid, and she lived and died with that clarity of personal identity.

## Our Identity as Leaders

As world-changing as Joan of Arc's mission was, it is only different in degree, not in kind, from that of every leader who has a vital work to do. Joan teaches us a few insights for managing our identity as leaders.

First, we must learn to use symbolism adroitly in leadership. Symbols proclaim identity and mission without words. Everyone is familiar with the happy "smile" that runs across the bottom of the Amazon logo. It is a pleasant symbol with a charitable giving program named after it. Yet, someone once explained to me that the left corner of the Amazon smile touches the first "A" of the name and then extends to the right corner which touches the "Z" in Amazon. In other words, the smile symbolizes that Amazon "sells everything from A-Z" – and we all know that to be true!

Symbols, because they are the universal language of humanity, are very versatile and have many uses: for company identity (logos, slogans, badges); to create feel and atmosphere (colors, banners, decorations); to communicate vitality (mascots, uniforms, music); to console and congratulate (medals, gifts, tokens of appreciation). The tractability and wide recognition of symbols are indications that the human person is made to communicate identity through symbols.

Second, symbols often point to a very personal identification with the thing symbolized: clergymen and nuns wear religious habits, preachers carry bibles, all manner of military and public service officials wear uniforms. The symbols tell others who the symbol-bearers are in subtle or overt ways. I once sat in an aisle seat on an airplane next to a cello strapped into the middle seat. The instrument's owner sat by the window, and I didn't need to ask him what he did for a living. Some symbols literally *shout* identity.

Like Joan, we must be very deliberate in displaying symbols for public consumption. Our symbols must never be false or deceptive. They must always express who we really are, but at times they can be reflective of values we *aspire to*, even if we have not quite arrived at the perfection of our desire. (Consider the adolescent who wears the jersey of his favorite NFL quarterback.) Our symbols always tell others who we are and what we value.

The third and final point is quite obvious. If we don't own our identity in the face of challenges, we will never be effective leaders. This is not a call to insist on always being right or to be overbearing with co-workers. It is a statement of fact. Strong leaders have strong identities. Your enemies will test you through slander and attack; your friends will test you through criticism, backbiting, and at times betrayal; your admirers will often project onto you *what they want you to be* and will be easily disillusioned if you don't live up to their sometimes unrealistic expectations.

No matter. All these challenges go with the territory. Be the leader *God* wants you to be. Own your identity.

Hold your banner high and charge into battle.

# 3

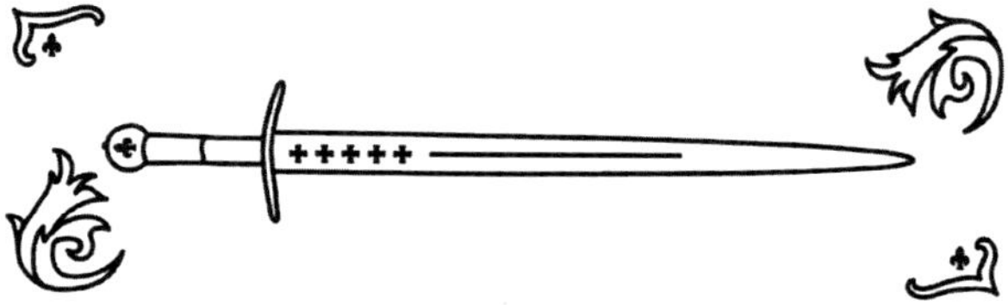

## THE SWORD

**<u>Virtue</u>: Power**

"I bring a message from *La Pucelle*," said the emissaries to the abbot of the monastery.

"I have heard tell of her claims to be the Maid who will save France," responded the aged monk with a gentle nod. "What is her request?"

"The Maid respectfully asks Your Reverence to remove the stones from the back of the sanctuary behind the altar, and digging, you will find there a sword imprinted with *fleurs-de-lis* and having five crosses on the blade. When you have done so, we are to bring the sword to the Maid for lifting the siege of Orléans."

"She wants me to *dig up the church sanctuary* to find a buried sword?!" exclaimed the cleric. "What an odd request!"

"Nevertheless, it must be done! So orders the Maid." The priest in charge of the Shrine of St. Catherine of Fierbois reluctantly called in several men who carried out the Maid's strange appeal only to find it just as she had said. The workers dug up from below the altar a rusty old sword that had seen better days. But the *fleurs-de-lis* – the symbol of France – were evident. And when they removed the light coating of rust – behold! – five crosses were etched on the blade.

### A New Savior of France Arises

As Joan of Arc was making the eleven-day trip on horseback through enemy territory to meet the future king of France, she paused her retinue to send emissaries to the local shrine to retrieve the sword whose existence beneath the altar had been hidden for six hundred years. (The fictional dialogue above may have captured something of the surprise of this extraordinary request and discovery.)

No one really knows how the sword got there, but God knew, and the patron saint of that shrine, St. Catherine of Alexandria, was one of Joan's voices who told the Maid that the sword had belonged to none other than the founding father of the French nation, Charles Martel. The great military leader is known to history as "the Hammer" for his stunning victory over the Saracens at the Battle of Poitiers in AD 732. Martel definitively ended the invasion of Muslims into France and became the first ruler of a united French people.

When it was revealed that Joan of Arc had miraculously discovered the treasure of the ancient sword, it was as if lightning had flashed across the whole of

Northern France. "The sword of Charles Martel has been uncovered! It is a miracle! The Maid has done it!" A tsunami of enthusiasm engulfed the French people to take back their nation.

Let us acknowledge three notable characteristics of leadership represented by the sword of Martel; continuity, double-edged power, and *tour de force* momentum.

⚜ Continuity:

When a dictator takes over the reins of power in a country (business, organization, etc.) he throws out all that came before him and begins the new regime with himself. *His* ideology and power structure will henceforth reign. Tyrants do that, but real leaders do not. Yes, oftentimes changes must be made and reforms undertaken, particularly when a new leader takes over a struggling institution, but that is different from throwing out the baby with the bathwater and remaking an organization in one's own image and likeness. Good leaders are like the master of the household that Jesus spoke of in the Gospel, who can "bring out of his storehouse both the old and the new" (Matthew 13:52).

The resurrecting of Charles Martel's sword for the purpose of (once again) saving France from a hostile invasion was a brilliant stroke of leadership continuity. Wielding the *exact* sword that once belonged to the first savior of the French nation, Joan let the potent symbol of war do the talking:

"A new savior of France has arisen." Nor did she attempt to usurp power with the sword. On the contrary, she proclaimed her dying allegiance to the very monarchy of which Martel's famous grandson, Charlemagne, was the progenitor. Joan's use of power was remarkably balanced given she had no prior experience of politics or war.

Granted, no human wisdom could have discovered the sword's whereabouts, but God, who saw French history at a glance, from Charles Martel to Charles VII (Joan's king), also knew a leader when He saw one. To Joan he entrusted the potent symbol of power.

⚜ Double-Edged:

The sword is an apt metaphor for power. A sword may be used to kill an enemy or to block the blow of the enemy who is trying to kill you. Power is both coercive and protective, although a tyrant will only use his power to bend others to his will.

Joan knew how to utilize both edges of the blade of power. She relentlessly drove against her enemies with all the force provided by the political and military leaders of the day. In her first letter to the English commander she demanded that every Englishman leave France and promised retribution for their French collaborators if they continued to betray her beloved nation: "If you do not do so, I am commander of the armies, and in whatever place I shall meet your French allies, I shall make them leave it, whether they wish to or not; and if they will not obey, I shall have them all killed." Clearly, this was a woman who wielded power with enormous confidence.

There is also a humorous anecdote (unconfirmed by any serious historical record) that Joan broke the blade of Charles Martel's sword over the back of one of the "ladies of the night" when she drove out the prostitutes who shadowed the soldiers' camps looking for business. Sword in hand, Joan meant business.

At the same time, she balanced her coercive threats with reasonable allowances for her enemies to voluntarily retreat, which they rarely did. Also, wherever possible in the course of war, she forbade the victorious French troops from slaughtering their enemies. Joan used the double-bladed sword of power skillfully.

⚜ Tour de Force:

Power in leadership also has an emotional aspect. A leader's use of power can enthuse or depress his people depending upon whether it is used for service or selfish/ideological purposes. On the negative side, abuse of power corrupts and destroys. On the positive side, power accumulates with added victories and can create a sort of *tour de force* momentum in followers for the accomplishment of even greater victories that would not be possible in the early part of a campaign.

After Joan and her troops lifted the siege of Orléans in May of 1429, the French were almost unstoppable. Their victories had created an emotional momentum for the French that also discouraged and intimidated the English. Joan then undertook a campaign in the Loire valley conquering one enemy-held city after another from Orléans to the kingly city of Reims (165 miles apart). The dauphin could only be crowned at Reims, and a *tour de force* military campaign was the only way to get him there through hostile lands.

The exercise of power *in victory* is also a leadership challenge. A victorious leader often attributes his successes to his own virtue and intelligence rather than to other decisive elements. In this, Joan showed herself a leader par excellence. Though decidedly proud of the French victories, she also gave exclusive credit to God and to her soldiers.

### Our Continuity in Leadership

Few of us will carry out military campaigns like Joan of Arc. But all of us exercise power in some way in our lives, even if that power is just our parental authority over children. It is *real* power, both coercive and protective, and it must be used properly.

First, we must always recognize the source of our power, which may have both natural and divine aspects. A true vocational calling has its origin in God's will, above all, but other humans always contribute to our formation as leaders as well. It is commonly said that "we stand on the shoulders of giants" in leadership. Many have gone before us and have given us the wisdom that helps us do our jobs properly.

As leaders in our own realms, we need to read, to ask questions, to consult, and to seek the wisdom of the ages to become a better servant of those entrusted to our care. Those who take over the leadership of institutions, churches, and businesses must be diligent to learn the "institutional history" of the organization, its founder, and of prior generations of leadership to assure continuity with the good things that have made that community what it is today.

Second, tyranny is not leadership. Leave the need for self-affirmation in the therapist's office and dedicate yourself to using the powers of *your office* (whether in a family or an organization) in a balanced way. Power is a creative force that acts as a conduit to progress and reform. It is also protective, a means to guard from attacks and abuses. Use power for *them*, not for you.

Third, stay with the plan. The judicious exercise of creative power over a longer timeframe often has a cumulative effect on those who have a stake in the mission. Victories create excitement and momentum for accomplishing even greater goals, as long as the leaders don't let things go to their heads or abuse their power.

Pick up your sword and go from victory to victory, and you will learn the transformative nature of power when used for all the right things in leadership.

# 4

# THE HORSE

## Virtue: Mobility

It must have been a magnificent creature.

The horse given to Joan of Arc by the Duke of Lorraine was not a battle-horse, a mighty steed, but a smaller charger – sleek, agile, quick as lightning, and beautiful. The diminutive Maid would not have even been able to handle one of the great war horses! But she immediately took to her dark-coated charger and made him her own. From that day, they became united in the same mission to save France. Her family did not own a horse, and it is not clear whether Joan had ever ridden one before she received this gift from the Duke, but when she hopped on her charger, a hidden natural gift of horsemanship came to life in her. God knew what she needed for her mission. She needed to be mobile.

### Mobility as a Leadership Asset

Joan once said, given her natural inclinations, she would much rather have remained back in her village taking care of domestic chores than be out on a battlefield. One can understand that sentiment in a teenage girl called to extraordinary feats and sacrifices. Yet, she had to go where God wanted her to go, and she needed transportation to get there.

All leaders of any stripe need to be mobile. Mobility is a leadership asset, not a weakness. Leaders live within a very small comfort zone as the demands of their office call them to go out of themselves constantly and to connect with others for the mission. Travel is often difficult and disruptive. It usually causes frustration and demands great sacrifices of time and energy. Pope John Paul II, who was quite a dynamo himself, once commented that it is impossible for a modern leader *not* to be a traveler.

Travel and mobility are not the same thing. While physical travel is the essential component of this leadership virtue, mobility has a more expansive meaning with effects interpreted through dynamism, balance, and progress.

⚜ Dynamism:

A leader's movement is dynamic, purposeful, and ordered. The very perception of movement often gives vitality to a leader's mission and engenders dynamism in one's co-workers. Joan of Arc seemed to have an intuitive grasp of this when she traversed the entire length of Northern France on horseback several times in a few months. This was six hundred years before modern transportation made that an easy feat. Prior to that, Joan had never left the confines of her local community.

Have you ever noticed that the best leaders seem to be everywhere? Mobility keeps leaders in contact with their people. Allies in the mission need to see the leader in front of them regularly and in dynamic ways. The leader's presence engenders trust and enthusiasm. Certainly, office duties and boring in-house meetings are essential elements of leadership too, but the greatest leaders rally their people by going *to* them. Their connectedness and visibility create cohesion for the mission and its various parts.

⚜ Balance:

In this method, do not be deceived into believing you must be continuously mobile, as if being in perpetual motion were a leadership trait. It is not. Movement in leadership always has a purpose. The leader goes to his people for distinct reasons: to fulfill promises, to exhort, to encourage, to move the ball forward in some way. The great artistic representations of Joan since the 15th century most often show her riding into battle on her charger (usually depicted romantically as a white steed), fighting alongside her troops and encouraging them in the hard work of sacrifice for a greater cause.

At the same time, movement for the sake of movement serves no useful purpose. Mobility's purpose is both creative and protective. Leaders must discern carefully when to move, where to move, and how best to move an organization, an army, or a family. In his recent book, *Christus Vincit*, the Archbishop of Kazakhstan, Athanasius Schneider, told the story of his father's decision to move the family from a stable situation in their native Kyrgyzstan to the country of Estonia, hundreds of miles away. The father's reason for moving: he feared that if the family stayed in place, his children would be indoctrinated as Communists and lose their souls. This is true parental leadership with mobility as the servant.

⚜ Progress:
The greatest leaders often impress their subordinates with their enormous energy for a cause. They do not allow grass to grow underfoot, as the saying goes, and people get swept up in their resolute movement – sometimes to the point of exhaustion! Subordinates often complain that they can't keep up with their boss. So be it. A commitment is a commitment. It demands a great deal of a leader's energies, but such dynamism also has great effect. The famous scholar Joseph Campbell once pointed out that "the influence of a vital person *vitalizes*."

This was certainly the case with Joan of Arc who announced her mission objectives to friends and foes alike and relentlessly pursued them. Her vast resources of vital energy drew kings, nobles, armies, whole towns and even *nations* in her wake. But her movement was focused and always undertaken in pursuit of a singular goal. She illustrated Campbell's vital principle: her movement which was directed toward tangible progress for the good of others *vitalized* everyone around her.

## Our Movement as Leaders

Gone are the days of warfare on horseback, but the need for mobility in pursuit of a cause remains. Mobility is a staple of all leadership, and we must manage our movements well if we are to be effective leaders.

First, our movement has to be creative and dynamic. Our leadership responsibilities may not require us to travel out of our local area, but they will always require "travel" out of one's comfortable routine. A father's sacrifice to take off work early to be physically present at his child's soccer game or school event, for example, is dynamic leadership mobility of the most important kind. It puts the right values first and organizes around those values. And the decisions about mobility are situational. Each leader tailors his mobility to his own unique circumstances with the understanding that he moves purposefully for the good of others.

Second, perpetual motion machines are not leaders. Leaders are balanced between movement and stillness, and they know the value of each. Like the musical score that features strong movements punctuated by pauses and deliberate silences, we must also rest from our hectic activities from time to time. Jesus periodically invited His disciples to "come out of the way and rest for a while" (Mark 6:31) in order for them to appreciate the leadership value of both activity and rest.

Third, let your leadership – and life – be one of continuous progress in the good. The famous management expert, Peter Drucker, once posed a question that every leader should ask himself: "When you look back on your life, what do you want to be remembered for?" Certainly, leadership is not a matter of building up one's ego. It is a matter of moving the world.

Go, plunge into the mission on your horse and change the world.

# 5

# THE ARMOR

**Virtue: Realism**

Cutting her hair and donning men's clothes to fit in with her male counterparts was not enough. Medieval warfare contained all kinds of drastic killing and ripping instruments that tore flesh and pierced bodies. Even before her first battle, Joan of Arc understood enough about the challenges of war to know that she needed protection.

A tailor-made set of armor was crafted by the dauphin's armorers to fit the special contours of the maiden's form. It must have been the most extraordinary suit of armor ever created! It is one of the greatest tragedies of history that Joan's armor has never been recovered.

Her suit of armor was reportedly white. In the thick of battle, it gave Joan the menacing look of a medieval warrior princess.

## Realism as Essential to Success

It is readily acknowledged by most historians that some of Joan's early bursts of enthusiasm for her mission were not based on solid military wisdom. When she first approached the city of Orléans, for example, she wanted to attack a fortified outpost of the English with only a fraction of the troops her enemy had. Hers were untrained and untested. Had the battle-hardened commander, John of Dunois, not exercised his veto power at that moment, Joan of Arc might be a footnote in the history books!

Realism about *actual* circumstances of our world (and of our enemies) is essential to success in a mission. Some leaders like Joan of Arc show extraordinary charisma and judgment in their given missions, but no leader is endowed with tested wisdom from the beginning, and even great ones like Joan need to develop realism for their respective battles.

Let us acknowledge three notable characteristics of Joan's leadership realism: protection, insight, and limitations.

⚜ Protection:

Joan of Arc wore armor to protect her from arrows and other lethal projectiles hurled against her by a ferocious enemy. She, as the inspirational leader, was their ultimate target. Joan fought in more than a dozen engagements against her foes in only a few months' time. We can only imagine how often the English soldiers tried to kill the Maid whose very existence was a mortal threat to their plans.

Joan was realistic about the dangers of warfare and secured a very personal sort of protection. Even then, armor didn't fully prevent injury, but it did save her life more than once. In fact, in her first major clash with the English before the walls of Orléans, Joan was injured by an arrow that penetrated the seams of her armor and drove through her chest so far that the point protruded out of her back. When the battlefield medics were debating how to best help her, she simply pulled the arrow out with her own hand. (Now there's a leadership challenge!)

We know of at least three other injuries that Joan sustained in war (an arrow to the thigh, a stone dropped on her head from above, and stepping on one of those medieval spiked metal balls on a chain). But Joan knew that all leadership comes with risks and that no armor plating on earth can protect a leader from every possible danger. Good leaders are steeped in realism about the deadly threats they face and take measures to protect their persons, their assets, and their people.

⚜ Insight:

We don't often get a realistic picture of our challenges without taking time out to contemplate the scenarios before us. Leaders must consult and strategize with their teams, of course, but above all, realism requires personal brain power.

Leaders must sit down and think about their challenges and evaluate all factors as a prelude to any course of action.

And sometimes your thoughtful ideas will be at odds with those who are less insightful or overly cautious. After the French lifted the siege of Orléans, Joan looked carefully at her enemy's capabilities and discerned their essential weakness: the English were overextended, inattentive to the threat, and arrogant. Joan's allies didn't pay attention to those vulnerabilities, however, and were inclined to let the troops rest a few days after their victory at Orléans.

Joan had greater insight and ordered an attack.

The lopsided war that ensued in a field called Patay, just north of Orléans, proved to be the death blow to the English presence in that region and the beginning of the end of their occupation of France. The French killed 2,000 English soldiers in battle that day and lost only *three*. There is no substitute for intelligent realism in leadership.

⚜ Limitations:

A suit of armor is both protective and confining. Joan's first major English foe, Commander William Glasdale, died in a watery grave because he could not extricate himself from his heavy armor when he fell off a burning bridge at Orléans.

Despite her divine calling to lead armies, Joan didn't have *actual* command of the French troops. She often found herself in a subordinate position of power and limited by the existing military command structure. Her victories are all the more incredible given her real limitations in politics and warfare.

Neither did she hold perfect sway over the dauphin who, as is well-attested by his biographers, was prone to fits of sincere enthusiasm counterbalanced by inexcusable resistance to her plans depending on who was whispering in his ear at the time. Joan expressed enormous frustration that the king, once crowned, would not immediately march on the city of Paris, yet, she ultimately obeyed his command to come off the battlefield and let the insufferable politicians try to work out a diplomatic solution.

Leaders see what is possible and respect what is not possible in the circumstances of their leadership situation. They live within their realistic limitations and live to fight another day.

## Our Realism as Leaders

Leadership realism is a function of experience, engaged intelligence, consultation with advisors, and a willingness to admit limits. No one is born with all these capacities; we must develop them through time and experience. Here are the essentials for developing realism in leadership:

First, personal protection is essential in wars and competitions of any type, but a leader also protects his people and his assets. If your enemy takes away your weapons to fight him, he has already won. If your enemy takes out your *people*, he has weakened your ability to make war. Accomplishing anything of value requires risk, the expenditure of resources and personnel, etc. Sometimes leaders make great sacrifices yet still lose. No good leader, however, puts his person, his people, or his resources at *unnecessary* risk.

Second, spend time every single day seriously contemplating how best to do your mission, how to improve it, how to become more effective at it, both quantitatively and qualitatively. Spend resources for training and equipment (like armor), both for yourself and for your people, with the understanding that training gives everyone a more realistic view of the job. Reliable equipment also helps us meet our realistic challenges with confidence. We owe our very best efforts to God and to our people in carrying out the mission entrusted to us. The old military saying applies to every leader: the soldier has a right to good leadership. His life depends on it.

Third, accept your limitations and your inevitable mistakes. Don't lament them, learn from them. You cannot avoid them, but you can transform them into wise realism. Be patient and prudent, and keep trying.

Call to mind that young woman who wanted to attack a fortress unprepared. She wisely learned from the old battle axe, Dunois, and eventually conquered the world's most formidable army.

# 6

## THE FEMININE

**Virtue: Attraction**

"A virgin has arisen from Lorraine and is laying claim to the ancient legend that prophesied the end of English domination in France. She says she is going to lift the siege of Orléans! What shall we do?"

This was the quandary that greeted the future king one day when he asked his chief chamberlain for news of his realm. I'm sure there has never been a more electrifying message to cross the desk of a powerful man. A maiden? A warrior? Defeat the English? Charles was intrigued to say the least, and with him, all of France.

At age seventeen Joan set out to meet the dauphin petitioning the local constable, a man named Robert de Baudricourt, for help in getting to the royal palace. Baudricourt was a former military man who kept the lid on a fragile order in the Lorraine region for many years and was known to the dauphin. Joan had no resources of her own to undertake this mission so it was up to Baudricourt to get her there.

Not unexpectedly, the constable rudely turned her away and told the uncle who had brought her to take her back home and give her a good spanking.

But Joan of Arc's mission was afoot, and her feminine genius was not to be deterred.

About that same time, French troops had just suffered a catastrophic defeat in their first attempt to liberate Orléans from the siege, and Joan received a highly specific revelation about the event. Soon after, she returned to Baudricourt and told him he was *personally responsible* for the deaths of their countrymen while he had in his hands the solution to the crisis and did nothing.

That got the military man's attention.

The young woman persevered in her demand, insisted on it with intensity, and may have even pointed a finger in the constable's face as she spoke. Had *a man* acted that way toward the grizzled commander, Baudricourt would have lopped off his head.

Lo and behold! Joan got her ticket to the royal court.

### The Unique Power of the Feminine

In the modern age we are accustomed to seeing women in leadership roles, but the societies of the Middle Ages were most definitely *not*. Certainly, there were famous and even powerful women in public life in that era, but when Joan, the maiden from rural France, declared that she was chosen to save the country by leading an army, she shocked the nation.

Her vibrant femininity, so suddenly intruding into the stark world of men, was one of those mighty, natural gifts she traded on to enhance the mission.

Joan utilized two powerful characteristics of femininity to serve her mission well: total beauty and magnetism.

⚜ Total Beauty:

Interestingly, there are no contemporaneous witnesses who praise Joan's *physical beauty* – those were the embellishments of later legends about her – but she was undoubtedly lovely in the way that any maiden in the flower of her youth would be. Her *femininity*, however, was another matter. When men of the 15th century wanted to laud a woman's beauty, they did it in a characteristically medieval way: they praised her *purity*. Their evaluation of beauty went much deeper than the surface aspects of things (and moderns could learn a lot from them in that regard). A woman's virtue was the source of her credibility. To "prove" herself, Joan had to undergo several humiliating virginity tests (conducted by noble women) and had to maintain the high moral standards of her faith and culture for her gender.

The excellence of Joan's moral character is so fully documented as to be indisputable. This may be why she had such a purifying effect on the soldiers she lived and fought with at close quarters. It seems to have been a consensus of all of her male associates that they felt not the slightest temptation to impurity when they were in her presence. In fact, her closest advisor, Jean, Duke of Alençon, once testified, without a hint of exaggeration, that Joan was the most virtuous (in his terms, *purest*) woman on the face of the earth.

The universal recognition of her total womanly beauty and high moral character gave Joan a unique leverage over men that a male could not possibly have had over other men of action. It is hard to overestimate the fervor with which the men of her day greeted the Maid and embraced her mission. When Joan set out to lift the siege of Orléans, the dauphin could barely muster 2,000 straggling recruits to accompany her. When she rode into the city of Reims for the king's coronation less than three months later more than 11,000 soldiers rode with her.

⚜ Magnetism:

Added to her natural attractiveness, Joan's absolute conviction about her mission and her ability to articulate the terms of it drew men to her like a magnet. One historian called this the "irresistible power of her presence", which we can imagine was a combination of her recognized beauty and the force of her personality. While she did have extraordinary spiritual gifts (like prophecy and insight into souls) her personal magnetism seemed to be a very natural quality that Joan used well for her mission.

For example, despite her total lack of formal education (she could not even read), Joan was extremely sharp-witted, and by all accounts was masterful in her use of the French language and imagery. Her exhortations delivered in a youthful soprano voice, her petite stature (at least compared to the men around her), and her rousing, emotional appeals for France made Joan's femininity a powerful weapon of attraction.

Her personality was so dynamic and her words so persuasive that even cynical, worldly men fell under her spell. A French nobleman, Constable Arthur de Richemont, who had previously betrayed the French king, was so taken by Joan that he renounced his service to England and rejoined the king's cause. Richemont provided the military force that ultimately proved decisive to drive out the English.

At the risk of being accused of sexism, we may say that Joan's feminine magnetism had an overwhelmingly motivating power over the demoralized men – and nation – of her day. It is unlikely that even a handsome young man in the vigor of his youth could have had the same effect. Joan's feminine beauty and virtue simply won over the hearts of her countrymen.

## The Power of Attraction in Leadership

Natural attractiveness and personal dynamism are not only female traits, but Joan shows us how *any* inherent human characteristics can be used for leadership. *Everyone* has some force of personal attraction to use for their mission. Here, of course, we are referring only to entirely moral and proper ways of exercising personal influence. As with Joan, a leader's credibility has a great deal to do with personal integrity and a high standard for moral character.

Beauty is the first attraction over the hearts and minds of others, yet not in a physical way. Wherever some human skill or capacity is well-developed and well-utilized for a distinct purpose, we see real beauty. I recall watching a friend of mine sit at my computer and, in the space of about ten minutes, he adroitly fixed a technical problem that had plagued me for months. In addition to being very grateful, I was overwhelmed by his amazing technical knowledge and proficiency, which were utterly outside my skill set. In a very literal sense, my friend's simple act was a beautiful thing to behold.

The same dynamic expresses itself when people act virtuously, when they accomplish great tasks with skill, or when they perform brilliantly at anything. These gifts are immensely attractive and draw people to them. I once interviewed the '90s country music star, Collin Raye, who told me that his calling to be a professional musician came when he went to see the rock band, the Eagles, in concert. He was so deeply affected by their performance that he made a decision right then and there to live the rest of his life performing music like his heroes on stage. His particular pathway to his dream eventually led to country music, but the attraction to the life of a performing musician was instilled in his heart at a rock concert.

We must also recognize that at times the unique contributions of women around us remain underutilized for our missions. When President John F. Kennedy made an official state visit to France in the early sixties, he knew how important it was to first win over the hearts of the French people. Upon arrival in Paris, he asked his lovely wife, Jackie – who spoke fluent French – to exit from Air Force One first, with JFK following behind her. Predictably, the image of the President's arrival emblazoned on the front page of every French newspaper that evening was of the elegant First Lady exiting the enormous airplane and greeting all the dignitaries in their native language – with her husband in tow. It was a huge PR *splash* with the French!

Secondly, a leader is "magnetic" when he or she has full conviction about the mission, well-honed skills for the task, and a persuasive ability to articulate the need that drives the mission. The average person is not attracted to flaccid leadership or to charlatans in corner offices. True leadership is not the ability to whip up a crowd or manipulate others into doing the leader's will. It is the ability to *draw* others to a cause and sustain them – morally, psychologically, even spiritually – as they see the mission through to its stated goals.

Joan had all of these abilities, gifts of both nature and spirit. *You* have some unique gifts and capacities for your mission too.

Go, use them to set the world on fire.

# 7

## THE AUTHORITY

**Virtue: Inspiration**

On April 29th, 1429 the Maid rode through the eastern Burgundy Gate of the city of Orléans – still under siege – accompanied by hundreds of her troops, with military commanders and adjutants at her side. Thousands of the hungry, frightened residents of the city lined up to joyfully greet the Maid as she swept into their town like a force of nature to let the people know that their cause was now engaged by a leader with real authority.

Nothing like that military parade had even been seen in the history of warfare. It was certainly not the largest military procession ever to take place, but it must have been a pageant of epic emotional and spiritual proportions.

The impressive French knights rode in on their war horses emblazoned with silky, colorful heraldry; the grim soldiers held their weapons aloft and sang songs from the heart of their homeland; and the famed Maid on her black charger, in gleaming armor, unfurled her twelve-foot banner in the wind to the wonderment of the entire city. She came by authority of the dauphin and in the names of Jesus and Mary.

All fear of a besieging enemy vanished.

### Authority Brings Hope

People will only follow leaders who give them hope. Superficial pleasures and passing fads play well in pop culture, but only for a time. When life's real challenges overwhelm people, they need inspiration to conquer their problems. Above all, they need hope to sustain them through what they cannot instantly change. Hope undoes the dominance of fear and conquers the hearts of people. Hope is the coin of the realm when dispensed by those who bear true authority. Joan of Arc's inspirational leadership offered hope to the people of France through her influence, heart, and pageantry.

⚜ Influence:

Leaders must be clear about the distinction between power and authority. Power comes through a commission or a public office of some kind. It usually has a legal character and some capacity to oblige people to do the leader's will. Authority, on the other hand, is not the same as power. It is influence. It has a *human* not an institutional face and operates through persuasion and the creative use of gifts.

While Joan of Arc had been designated by the dauphin to lift the siege of Orléans, she was, strangely, not given a formal commission or a title to go with it. The military commanders held all the *power*. But that did not stop Joan from exercising her enormous influence over the soldiers and political leaders of the day for the fulfillment of her mission.

Relatively few in life get to exercise real power. Everyone gets to exercise authority in their own realm.

⚜ Heart:

The purpose of authority is to capture the hearts of those being led and to form them into a coalition of the willing to undertake a noble cause. Joan had an immense capacity to speak to people's hearts and convince them of the need to join her in freeing France from the grip of an invading power. No one, not even the future king, thought such a thing was possible. But Joan's fervent authority made this goal not only thinkable, believable, and desirable – but *possible*.

How did she exercise her influence? First, she insisted that all soldiers and allies pray and convert their hearts to God as the only way to call down divine power in their cause. Then she roused them with every type of exhortation and inspirational speech, using imagery from the history of France (Charlemagne was her favorite) and the rich traditions of faith to inspire them.

Then, finally, she met her enemies and naysayers with rebukes and direct challenges (such as her feisty letters to the English mentioned in Chapter 2). When asked by a skeptical bishop if Michael the archangel spoke English when he appeared to her, Joan retorted: "Do you think the angels speak the language of *our enemies*?!" Spirited rhetoric like that always captures hearts and imaginations!

⚜ Pageantry:

No people on earth are more skilled at pageantry than the French, and Joan tapped that inspiring cultural wellspring for her cause. When pageantry is done well, it lifts people's spirits immensely. Imagine how many boys of Orléans wanted to run out and join the army right then, or how many girls wanted to become like that fascinating Maid the day Joan road through the gates of the city!

Pageantry offers creative possibilities for leaders everywhere: celebrations, rousing speeches, motivational talks, and even well-crafted gestures of personal encouragement. These serve to lift hearts, minds, and spirits for the greater cause. Joan was a master of these tools of influence and authority.

### The Call to Inspirational Leadership

Whenever I think of inspirational leaders, I vividly recall an incident as a student during a study program in Italy. That semester, I was able to secure tickets to an Easter Mass in St. Peter's Basilica in Rome. My mother and father were visiting, and we had the good fortune to obtain seats on the center aisle for the Mass. When Mass began, I recall watching Pope John Paul II walking slowly in procession up the aisle blessing everyone on both sides as he went. My mother also saw him coming toward us, and as the pope got progressively closer, she broke out in a torrent of tears. The beautiful music, the majestic setting, and above all, the very living presence of an authoritative man of God opened the floodgates of emotion for my mother that day. I could hardly keep from crying myself.

Joan of Arc must also have had that kind of emotional impact on the people of her day. But this incident shows the incredible power of inspirational authority in leadership.

First of all, authority well-carried is a very personal form of influence over others and has the capacity to touch their hearts without need for words. The authoritative person exudes an inspiration not only because of his great deeds, but primarily through his lived ideals. Few of us will ever rise to the heights of sanctity as Joan of Arc or Pope John Paul II, but all of us, as leaders, are called to pursue virtue as a way of life. Leadership without virtue quickly decays into tyranny. But leaders with humility and magnanimity of soul can literally transform the world.

Secondly, the influence wielded by an inspirational leader brings us back to where we began this book: spirit. *Inspiration* has "spirit" as its root. Pageantry in leadership is not about superficial festivities. It's about enabling the human spirit to express itself in meaningful, symbolic, and inspirational ways that give hope to the human heart, particularly in times of great desolation. Militaries have parades and award ceremonies; political parties hold conventions; motivational teachers create slogans and incentive programs to keep their charges motivated to fulfill their missions in and out of season.

Take a moment to imagine being a resident of Orléans in April of 1429 as Joan of Arc rode into your beleaguered town that was suffering from the months-long English siege. Then imagine how motivated *you* would have been to lift that siege and banish the invaders from your land.

## Conclusion

Alas, dear reader, we have come to the end of this book. In a few short pages we have discovered what kind of virtue motivates a true leader. We have seen those gifts displayed in their full regalia by a historical figure who lived them to the maximum.

My hope is that you have absorbed at least a spark of the spirit of the Maid of Orléans as sustenance for your own mission. You too have been called to lead others, and many souls depend upon your dynamic leadership to give them inspiration and hope.

Go now, lead a parade and change the world!

# BIBLIOGRAPHY

Mary Gordon, *Joan of Arc: A Life*, NY: Penguin Books, 2008.

Kathryn Harrison, *Joan of Arc: A Life Transfigured.* NY: Doubleday, 2014.

Régine Pernoud and Marie-Véronique Clin, *Joan of Arc: Her Story*, NY: St. Martin's Griffin, 1998.

V. Sackville-West, *Saint Joan of Arc*, NY: The Literary Guild, 1936.

Sven Stolpe, *The Maid of Orleans: The Life & Mysticism of Joan of Arc*, San Francisco: Ignatius Press, 2014.

Mark Twain, *Personal Reflections of Joan of Arc,* NY: Harper & Brothers, 1896.

**For Teens and Young Adults**

Kathleen Kudlinski, *Joan of Arc: A Photographic Story of a Life*, NY: DK Publishing, 2008.

Louis de Wohl, *Joan of Arc: Girl Soldier*, San Francisco: Ignatius Press, 2001.

# AUTHOR'S BIO

Peter Darcy is a writer and editor who spent thirty years in the non-profit sector and various business enterprises. He has travelled the world attempting to bring the Kingdom of Christ to others and is the founder of the "One Our Father" Prayer Campaign (www.oneourfather.com). He published *Mister Buddy's Guide to Non-Profit Leadership: Principles for Success in a Charitable World* (Tremendous Leadership) in 2019 and has authored or ghostwritten seven other books. Look for his full-length book, *Joan of Arc: Leader of Men,* to come out in 2021. Readers can contact him via email at peterdarcywriter@yahoo.com.

## Read more excellent titles from our Life-Changing Classics Series available at www.TremendousLeadership.com

***3 Therapies of Life (The),*** by Charlie "Tremendous" Jones; Foreword by Dr. Tracey C. Jones.

***7 Golden Rules of Milton Hershey (The),*** by Greg Rothman; Foreword by Richard Zimmerman.

***7 Leadership Virtues of Joan of Arc (The),*** by Peter Darcy.

***Acres of Diamonds,*** by Russell H. Conwell; Appreciation by John Wanamaker.

***Advantages of Poverty,*** by Andrew Carnegie; Foreword by Dale Carnegie.

***As a Man Thinketh,*** by James Allen.

***Books Are Tremendous,*** edited by Charlie "Tremendous" Jones; Introduction by J.C. Penney.

***"Bradford, You're Fired!",*** by William W. Woodbridge.

***Breakthrough Speaking,*** by Mark Sanborn.

***Character Building,*** by Booker T. Washington.

***Discipleship,*** by John M. Segal.

***From Belfast to Narnia: The Life and Faith of C.S. Lewis,*** by The C.S. Lewis Institute.

***Greatest Thing in the World (The),*** by Henry Drummond; Introduction by Dwight L. Moody.

***Key to Excellence (The),*** by Charlie "Tremendous" Jones.

***Kingship of Self-Control (The),*** by William George Jordan; Foreword by Charlie "T" Jones.

***Lincoln Ideals (The),*** edited by Charlie "Tremendous" Jones.

***Luther on Leadership,*** by Stephen J. Nichols.

***Maxims of Life & Business,*** by John Wanamaker; Forewords by Elbert Hubbard and Russell Conwell.

***Message to Garcia (A),*** by Elbert Hubbard.

***My Conversion,*** by Charles Spurgeon; Edited & Compiled by Charlie "T" Jones.

***Mystery of Self-Motivation (The),*** by Charlie "Tremendous" Jones.

***New Common Denominator of Success (The),*** by Albert E.N. Gray; Foreword by Charlie "Tremendous" Jones.

***Price of Leadership (The),*** by Charlie "Tremendous" Jones; foreword by Dr. Tracey C. Jones.

***Reason Why (The),*** by R.A. Laidlaw; Introduction by Marjorie Blanchard.

***Ronald Wilson Reagan: The Great Communicator,*** by Greg Rothman.

***Self-Improvement through Public Speaking,*** by Orison Swett Marden; Introduction by Forrest Wallace Cato.

***Science of Getting Rich: Abridged Edition (The),*** by Wallace D. Wattles; edited by Charlie "T" Jones.

***Succeeding With What You Have,*** by Charles Schwab; Foreword by Andrew Carnegie.

***That Something,*** by William W. Woodbridge; Introduction by Paul J. Meyer.

***Three Decisions (The),*** by Charlie "Tremendous" Jones; Foreword by Dr. Tracey C. Jones.

***Walt Disney: Dreams Really Do Come True!,*** by Jason Liller.

***Wit and Wisdom of General George S. Patton (The),*** compiled by Charlie "T." Jones.